Bibliographic information published by the German National Library:

The German National Library lists this publication in the National Bibliography; detailed bibliographic data are available on the Internet at http://dnb.dnb.de .

Imprint:

Copyright © 2017 GRIN Verlag
Print and binding: Books on Demand GmbH, Norderstedt Germany
ISBN: 9783668911758

This book at GRIN:

https://www.grin.com/document/461732

Haitham Ismail

Cloud computing. A security analysis

GRIN Verlag

GRIN - Your knowledge has value

Since its foundation in 1998, GRIN has specialized in publishing academic texts by students, college teachers and other academics as e-book and printed book. The website www.grin.com is an ideal platform for presenting term papers, final papers, scientific essays, dissertations and specialist books.

Security Analysis of cloud computing

By Haitham Ismail

Tables of Contents

List of Figures

A. Cloud computing definition

Traditionally, information technology infrastructure is designed based on maximum expected capacity. Afterwards, upgrade based on growth in usage or products end of life that require more start-up and operation cost, especially when it requires a team of experts to design and operate this infrastructure (Opusinteractive, 2017). However, Sviokla (2009) argues that IT services can be offered on-demand over a network including infrastructures, platforms, software (Daylmai, 2015) and services such as DOS filtration and security for emails through a data centres that are scattered all over the world called Cloud (Armbrust et al., 2010).

Mell and Grance (2011) state that cloud computing is enabling on-demand broad access over the network to computing resources such as servers, storage, applications and services that have the ability to be provisioned quickly with very low management overhead and provider interactions. However, payment is as the consumer uses from the resources depending on virtualizations and distributed technology (Dupré and Haeberlen, 2012).

In fact, cloud computing has many key players that carry out its maintenance and operations, such as, cloud consumer (CS) who is everyone that uses the cloud services as a customer; cloud provider (CSP) who makes cloud services available (Liu et al., 2011).

In addition, Hogan and Sokol (2013) state five essential characteristics of cloud computing.

> ➤ On-demand self-service: CS can self-provision the required computing resources (e.g. storage, memory, etc.) automatically without CSP interventions.

> ➤ Broad network access: Cloud services are offered over the network through thin or thick clients on any platforms (e.g. tablets, computers, etc.)

> ➤ Resource pooling: CSP shares his resources among multiple tenants who have different physical locations and demands that change rapidly by provisioning and de-provisioning the resources.

> Measured service: Cloud systems are measuring its services by metering the type of offered services (e.g. processing power, storage, etc.) that are monitored and reported in a transparent manner between CSP and CS.

> Rapid elasticity: computing power is elastic by which it can be provisioned and released automatically to server instantaneous demand by a way that appears to be ultimate.

In addition, as shown in the NIST special publication SP 800-145, Mell and Grance (2011) categorized cloud services into four different deployment models. First, private cloud by which cloud service provider CSP is offering the services to only one tenant that can be managed either by the provider or consumer. It can be on consumer premises or even outsourced private cloud. On the other hand, public cloud services are offered to different consumers. Third, the category is Community cloud is an infrastructure which is only used by a group of organisations share the same objectives (e.g. hospitals, banks). Finally, hybrid clouds are mixing different types of cloud in the same infrastructure. In addition, cloud computing is offered in three service models Dekker and Liveri (2015) mention that cloud services are offered in the following forms

> Infrastructure as a Service IaaS: Provider offers computing resources that are accessible online (e.g. online storage).

> Platform as a Service PaaS: Provider offers a platform (application servers) that consumer used to run their application on (e.g. Microsoft Azure).

> Software as a Service SaaS: Provider offers applications as a final product (e.g. Netflix)

B. The current adoption status of cloud computing by business organisations

Different size of organisations are interested in different services CSPs provide (e.g. IaaS, PaaS & SaaS), and this is due to the variation of resources, manpower and regulations, however, the degree of attraction varies between the different sizes of organisations. In addition, globalisation leads to the increase of the importance of cloud computing, for example, Companies regardless of their sizes, use and depend on cloud services for their business processes such as YouTube, Facebook, Twitter, etc. (Arı & Mardikyan, 2012).

There are many factors affecting the adoption process of cloud computing. According to Hsu and Lin (2016), these factors are categorized as technical, organisational and environmental factors. Some organizations have technical concerns and believe that the traditional IT storage solution is more secure than cloud computing. In fact, over 52% of security professionals have tracked many malware infections to a Software as a service application and they consider cloud computing as an infection vector (McAfee, 2016). Other factors affecting cloud adoption is the organisational factor. In small and medium size (SMB) organisation there is a lack of funding, resources and expertise which are the key reasons behind the faster rate of cloud adoption than the larger firms as the cloud adoption are relatively cheaper (Hsu & Lin, 2016). Furthermore, RightScale (2016) has developed a Cloud Maturity Model to classify and analyse organisations cloud usage and adoption level. This maturity model categorises the cloud consumers (CS) into

> ➢ Cloud Watchers: who have plans for cloud adoption but not yet have deployed any cloud application.

> ➢ Cloud Beginners: who are new in the field and seeking proof of concepts?

Security Analysis of cloud computing

➤ Cloud Explorers: who have already applications in the cloud and seeks to increase their dependency on cloud usage.

➤ Cloud Focused: who are in heavy use of cloud computing

In 2016, the percentage of Small & Medium that are cloud-focused (See Figure 1, Page 7) are 32% and almost 7% higher than the larger enterprise firms that have 25%. However, there is a growth of the number of the large Enterprises that are heavily utilising cloud (See Figure 2, Page

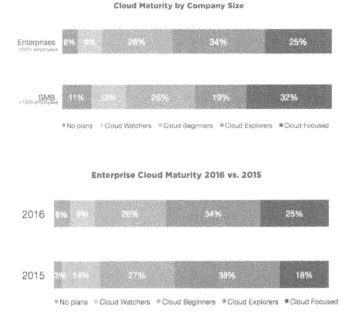

7) by 7% as they were only 18% in 2015, but in 2016, they become 25% (RightScale, 2016).

Figure 1 - Cloud Maturity level by company Size *(RightScale, 2016, p. 7)*

Figure 2 - Enterprise Cloud Maturity 2016 Vs. 2015 (RightScale, 2016, p. 7)

7

In 2016, the most used deployment model used by cloud-focused organizations are a hybrid

cloud by over 57% (McAfee, 2016; RightScale, 2016). However, private cloud only consumers

are dropped from 30% in 2015 to 19% in 2016 (McAfee, 2016) which indicate that the

consumers are not depending only on public cloud to support their business, instead, they are

using private cloud technologies besides it. According to McAfee (2016), this shift towards

hybrid computing is associated by strong demand on PaaS which currently occupy 40% of the

cloud consumers with a rise of 19% (See Figure 3, Page 8) from the last year.

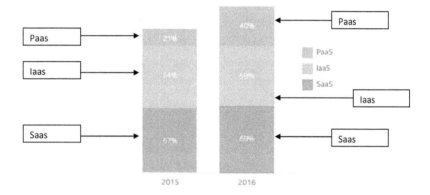

Figure 3 - Cloud services used in organisations (McAfee, 2016, p. 16)

In addition, organisational culture is one of the factors that are affecting cloud adoption. Arı &

Mardikyan (2012) state that cultural change is required, as by using cloud computing, the

concept of the ownership of the information systems will be changed. Indeed by cloud, Sivokla

(2009) mentioned that IT services like storage, communication, and application are not

necessarily connected to a device in front of you, instead, it can be provisioned on demand across

a network or the internet (Daylami, 2015). Finally, Hsu & Lin (2016) mentioned that

Environmental factors are one of the major factors that can affect cloud adoption. One example

8

of that is the competition of the market and how the organisations are affected by their competitor behaviour (e.g. offering services to customers using cloud services). Besides, some regulations might force some organisations to share information among competitors over a private cloud shared for that purpose.

In conclusion, there are factors that affect the cloud adoption of organisations (See Figure 5, Page 9). In addition, the most used deployment model in cloud computing is a hybrid cloud (See Figure 4, Page 9) or in another world a mix between private and public cloud deployment model. Furthermore, the most service model used is PaaS. However, SMB is more using cloud services more than larger Enterprises (See Figure 1, Page 7). On the other hand, there is a growth of the client-focused consumer of the large enterprise over the past year (See Figure 2, Page 7).

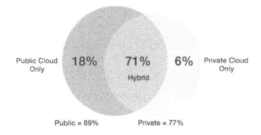

Figure 4 - The deployment model used by the organisation (RightScale, 2016, p. 9)

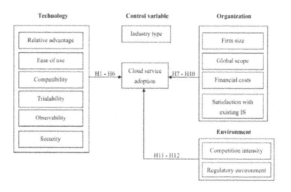

Figure 5 - Factors affecting cloud computing adoption (Hsu & Lin, 2016, p. 798).

C. Vulnerability and top threats.

Cloud computing is built based upon a concept of sharing resources among many consumers in a multitenant environment which is associated with many security risks (Dupré & Haeberlen, 2012). For example, in SaaS model, Cloud Consumers CS stores data within a shared application at the same network location with appropriate permission between CS and CSP, but if any exploits from one of the tenants or provider or even attacker, unauthorised access will take place (Gordon, 2016).

In fact, there are three types of risks that are associated with cloud adoption and they are policy and organisational risk, technical risk and legal risk, furthermore, each type risk has a probability of occurrence, impact to business and level of risk (Dupré & Haeberlen, 2012). First, Policy and organisational risk contain several subcategories that might include

> Vendor Lock-in: When using services from a provider that are built on provider property standard and not the international one, the vendor will be completely

dependent on a CSP's services and it will be difficult for a CS to move to another provider (Satzger, et al, 2013). For example, Application lock-in, SaaS provider offer application that is designed especially to their target market needs which means that custom database schema is developed that requires the CSP to develop a custom application that will read from this schema and prepare it for another provider schema in order to migrate (Dupré & Haeberlen, 2012).

➢ Loss of governance: By hosting Data at the cloud service provider data centres, cloud consumers abandon the control over the entire infrastructure to a third party, for example, provider might have prohibited port scanning, vulnerability assessments, penetration testing which consumer might need them in some cases to show due care and due diligence for ISO or PCI audit (Dupré & Haeberlen, 2012).

➢ Social Engineering attacks: Some administrative procedure such as creating user credentials happen via emails which might be subjected to spear phishing to get unauthorised access to these credentials (Dekker, M. & Liveri, 2015).

The second type of risks that are associated with cloud adoption according to Dupré & Haeberlen (2012):

➢ Resource exhaustion: Cloud computing is based on provisioning on-demand resources in a multitenant environment, and there is a probability that all tenants request high resources and provider could be not able to fulfil these needs which will cause service unavailability due to failure in delivery of the resources from the provider which could happen in peak resource usage (Dekker, M. & Liveri, 2015).

- ➢ Isolation failure: In a time of attacks, unauthorised access can take place due to exploits (Dupré & Haeberlen, 2012).

- ➢ Cloud provider malicious insider: Cloud provider's engineers have high privilege on their infrastructure that includes the infrastructure of tenants, so for example, there is a possibility of compromising consumers data by cloning it through IaaS virtual machine cloning (Nguyen, et al., 2014).

- ➢ Management interface compromise: Consumer management interface is given through web portable accessed through the internet (Dekker, M. & Liveri, 2015).

- ➢ Insecure deletion of data: Deleting data from the cloud storage does not mean that it is truly removed from the storage especially if the disk is not encrypted (Dupré & Haeberlen, 2012).

- ➢ Network attacks (e.g. DDOS): If one of the tenants is under a DDOS attack, the others tenants will be affected as they are both share the same resources (Dekker, M. & Liveri, 2015).

- ➢ Economic denial of service: Poor resource planning and miss-configuration can lead to a cost that is not affordable by the consumer (Dupré & Haeberlen, 2012).

- ➢ Software vulnerability: Using SaaS services which might have software vulnerabilities like SQL injection is crucial (Dekker, M. & Liveri, 2015)..

Finally, the legal risks are the same important as the other risks and it might include:

- ➢ Subpoena and e-discovery: Law enforcement officers might ask to provide information from the storage as evidence in criminal cases which can be provisioned to another cloud consumer (Dupré & Haeberlen, 2012).

> Risk of changing of jurisdiction: Information security related laws might be changing in the country of the provider or in the country of the consumers which might have an impact on security and privacy, besides, violation of this law by other consumers might lead the service to shut (Dekker, M. & Liveri, 2015).

> Data Protection Risks: Cloud computing is a concept that will make information to cross borders and data might be processed in another country which will make it difficult for data legalisation (Dupré & Haeberlen, 2012).

In conclusion, there are risks that are associated with cloud adoption that are classified into three categories. These risks have a probability of occurrence and impact on the business. Dupré & Haeberlen (2012) illustrate that a risk assessment should be done by the company or the organization to decide the risk treatment plan and based on that a decision is taken about what to adopt and what services to use in cloud

D. Prospective security measures that can enhance cloud adoption

According to Cloud Security Alliance (2009), organisations should conduct risk assessments for their services to take a decision of its adoption or not that should include asset evaluation, threats and vulnerabilities identifications, and their impact on the business process. After identifying risks and vulnerabilities that are associated with the cloud adoption, the risk treatment plan should be formulated and followed by risk monitoring to make sure the impact of the risk in an acceptable level from the business point of view (Hausman, et al., 2013).

Kovács et al. (2013) argue that vulnerability scanner engine can be used as a monitoring tool which will all kind of vulnerabilities in cloud services. The scanner engine will keep track of all IP addresses and URL and the possible vulnerabilities that might be raised, and it will give us the opportunity to remediate and fix them. In addition, all type of auditing logs generated from applications, platforms and infrastructure in cloud can be collected by security information and event management (SIEM) that will Analyse and correlate logs which in return will give visibility regarding our security posture in cloud, besides, it can be used to provide evidence in compliance reporting (Stephenson, 2014), besides by SIEM, there is an opportunity to have real-time malicious activity monitoring and incidents response options.

In addition, there are security controls and measures that information security specialists can take to protect their information in the cloud. In the risk assessment part, data classification should be done and select what could be suitable to be adopted in private cloud and what for public cloud, for example, sensitive information can be adopted in private cloud and non-sensitive information can be adopted in public cloud (Winkler, 2011). The adopted data should be encrypted by using strong encryption (e.g. AES 128 bit) prior to outsourcing for protecting data privacy and confidentiality (Wang, et al., 2012).

Furthermore, the backup and restore procedure should be conducted and tested as the main part of business continuity planning with the least possible privilege for the cloud provider and the consumer (Gordon, 2016). In addition, it should be included in the service level of agreement between both parties. For example, snap shot can be restored for a virtual machine in the cloud to revert back to a previous functional state. Over and above, Cloud Network security must be one of the main security controls that should be taken in consideration while designing cloud security program, so that virtual firewalls and virtual intrusion prevention systems (vIPS) should be used to protect cloud infrastructure. He, et al (2014) states that it can be placed in three-way (See Figure , Page 15) in the cloud, first, it can be placed as Figure 7a as one virtual firewall in the hypervisor logically before the virtual switching infrastructure or physical which lack the

14

security between the virtual machines and same applies on the vIPS, but it consume limited resources if it is virtual or consume nothing if it is physical.

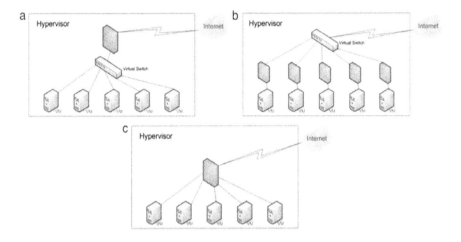

Figure 6 - Firewall implementation use cases in the Cloud (He, et al., 2014, p. 118)

Secondly, the design is based on a dedicated virtual firewall or vIPS (See Figure 6b, Page 154) for each virtual machine which will enhance the securities between hosted VM but it will heavily consume the hypervisor resources. Finally, to enhance security between the VMs and consume an acceptable level of resources from the hypervisor, security designers introduce one virtual firewall intercepting the traffic between all VMs (See Figure 6c, Page 14).

Policies of the firewall can be implemented in a way that will boost the performance and the throughput of the virtual firewall. He, et al (2014) introduce tree-rule firewall policy that has a tree execution design in a tree list (See Figure , Page 165) that will eliminate shadow policies and it will have faster execution.

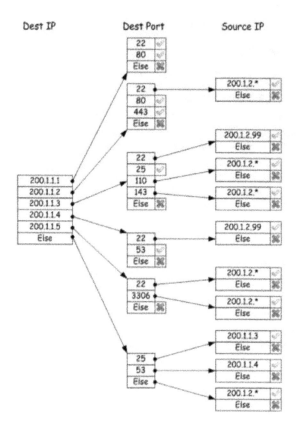

Figure 7 - Tree-Rule firewall rules design (He, et al., 2014, p. 121)

All of the security aspects should be discussed and agreed in a typical service level of agreement (SLA) that will define the cost, tasks and responsibilities for both the provider and the consumer as well, and it will include the privilege level for both parties, service monitor and reporting (Hausman, et al., 2013). In addition, data policies should be defined in the SLA including data protection, maintaining procedures, data location, data access and data transfer procedures (Gordon, 2016). Finally, there should be a state of transparency between the cloud providers and their consumers for announcing incidents and breaches.

Reference List

Arı, E. & Mardikyan, S., 2012. Factors Affecting the Adoption of Cloud Computing. Innovation Vision 2020: Sustainable growth, Entrepreneurship, and Economic Development, [Online],1(1), pp. 1094-1097.

Aleem, A. & Sprott, C. R., 2013. Let me in the cloud: Analysis of the benefit and risk assessment of cloud platform. Journal of Financial Crime, [Online], 20(1), pp. 6-24.

Armbrust, M, Fox, A, Griffith, R, Joseph, A, Katz, R, Konwinski, A, Lee, G, Patterson, D, Rabkin, A, Stocica, I, & Zaharia, M 2010, 'A View of Cloud Computing', Communications of the ACM, [Online], 53, 4, pp. 50-58

Cloud Security Alliance, 2009. Security Guidance for Critical Areas of Focus in Cloud Computing V2.1, [Online], US: Cloud Security Alliance CSA. Available at: https://cloudsecurityalliance.org/csaguide.pdf [Accessed 8 November 2016]

Daylami, N., 2015. The Origin and Construct of Cloud Computing. International Journal of the Academic Business World [Online], 9(2), pp.39-45.

Dekker, M. & Liveri, D., 2015. Cloud computing security risks and opportunities for SMEs, [Online] EU: European Union Agency for Network and Information Security (ENISA), Available at: https://www.enisa.europa.eu/publications/cloud-security-guide-for-smes/at_download/fullReport [Accessed 8 November 2016].

Dupré, L. & Haeberlen, T., 2012. Cloud computing benefits risks and recommendations for information security, [Online] EU: European Union Agency for Network and Information Security (ENISA), Available at: https://resilience.enisa.europa.eu/cloud-security-and-resilience/publications/cloud-computing-benefits-risks-and-recommendations-for-information-security [Accessed 16 June 2017].

Gordon, A., 2016. CCSP ISC2 Official Guide. 2 ed. New York: wiley, sybex.

Hausman, K., Cook, L., & Sampaio, T., 2013. Cloud Essentials: CompTIA Authorized Courseware for Exam CLO-001 (1), [Online] Somerset, US: Sybex. ProQuest ebrary. [Assessed at 7 December 2016].

Hogan, M. & Sokol, A., 2013. NIST Cloud Computing Standards Roadmap (NIST SP 500-291). [Online], Gaithersburg: U.S. Department of Commerce, Available at: https://www.nist.gov/sites/default/files/documents/itl/cloud/NIST_SP-500-291_Version-2_2013_June18_FINAL.pdf [Accessed 16 June 2017].

He, X., Chomsiri, T., Nanda, P. & Tan, Z., 2014. Improving Cloud network security. Future Generation Computer Systems, [Online], 30(1), pp.116-126

Hsu, C.-L. & Lin, J. C.-C., 2016. Factors affecting the adoption of cloud services in enterprises. Inf Syst E-Bus Manage, [Online],14, p.791–822.

Kovács, L., Kozlovszky, M., Törőcsik, M., Windisch, G., Ács, S., Prém, D., Eigner, G., Sas, P., 2013. Cloud security monitoring and vulnerability. IEEE 17th International Conference on Intelligent Engineering Systems, [Online], 1(1), pp.265 - 269.

McAfee, 2016. Building Trust in a cloudy sky, The state of cloud adoption and security. [Online] Available at: https://www.mcafee.com/us/resources/reports/rp-building-trust-cloudy-sky.pdf [Accessed 19 June 2017].

Mell, P. & Grance, T., 2011. The NIST definition of cloud computing (NIST SP 800-145), [Online], Gaithersburg: U.S. Department of Commerce, Available at: http://nvlpubs.nist.gov/nistpubs/Legacy/SP/nistspecialpublication800-145.pdf [Accessed 16 June 2017].

Nguyen, M.-D., Chau, N.-T., Jung, S. & Jung, S., 2014. A Demonstration of Malicious Insider Attacks inside Cloud IaaS Vendor. International Journal of Information and Education Technology, [Online], 4(6), pp. 483-486.

Opusinteractive, 2017. Cloud hosting vs traditional hosting. [Online] Available at: http://www.opusinteractive.com/cloud-hosting-vs-traditional-hosting/ [Accessed 8 July 2017].

RightScale, 2016. STATE OF THE Cloud Adoption. [Online] Available at: http://assets.rightscale.com/uploads/pdfs/RightScale-2016-State-of-the-Cloud-Report.pdf [Accessed 21 June 2017].

Satzger, B., Hummer, W., Inzinger, C.,Leitner, P. & Dustdar, S., 2013 "Winds of Change: From Vendor Lock-In to the Meta Cloud," in IEEE Internet Computing,[Online], 17(1), pp.69-73

Stephenson, P. 2014, "SIEM", SC Magazine, vol. 25, no. 4, pp.36.

Liu, F. Tong, J, Mao, Robert Bohn, Messina, J. Badger, L. & Leaf, D, 2011. Cloud Computing reference architecture (NIST SP 500-292), [Online], Gaithersburg: U.S. Department of Commerce, Available at: http://ws680.nist.gov/publication/get_pdf.cfm?pub_id=909505, [Accessed 8 November 2016].

Wang, C., Ren, K., Cao, N. & Lou, W., 2012. Enabling Secure and Efficient Ranked Keyword Search over Outsourced Cloud Data. IEEE transaction on parallel and distrubtion systems,[Online], 23(8), pp. 1467-1479.

Winkler, V., 2011. Securing the cloud. [Online] New Yourk: Elsevier Inc. Accessed 11 June 2017].

YOUR KNOWLEDGE HAS VALUE